EASY DIABETES COOKBOOK

1000+ Days of Easy and Delicious Diabetes Recipes with a 30-day Meal Plan to Manage Type 1 Diabetes, Type 2 Diabetes, and Borderline Diabetes for Beginners and Advanced Users

Dr. Raymond Harris

Copyright ©Dr.Raymond Harris,2023.

All rights reserved. No part of this publication may be reproduced, distributed, or transmitted in any form or by any means, including photocopying, recording, or other electronic or mechanical methods, without the prior written permission of the publisher, except in the case of brief quotations embodied in critical reviews and certain other noncommercial uses permitted by copyright law.

Table of content

INTRODUCTION
Brief Advice for newly diagnosed
Understanding Diabetes: A Brief Overview
Causes and Risk Factors
Common Symptoms
The Role of Exercise in Diabetes Management
Creating an Effective Exercise Routine
Chapter one :
Diabetes-Friendly Breakfasts
Chapter Two
Savory Lunch Creations
Chapter Three:
Delectable Dinners
Chapter four:
Satisfying Snacks

Chapter five
Diabetic-Friendly Desserts
Chapter six
Exercise Routines
moderate blood glucose and decrease tension
Chapter seven
Meal Planning and Portion Control
Managing Blood Sugar
Chapter Nine
Additional Resources
Conclusion
Embracing a Healthier Lifestyle with Diabetes
It Sample 30-Day Meal Plan

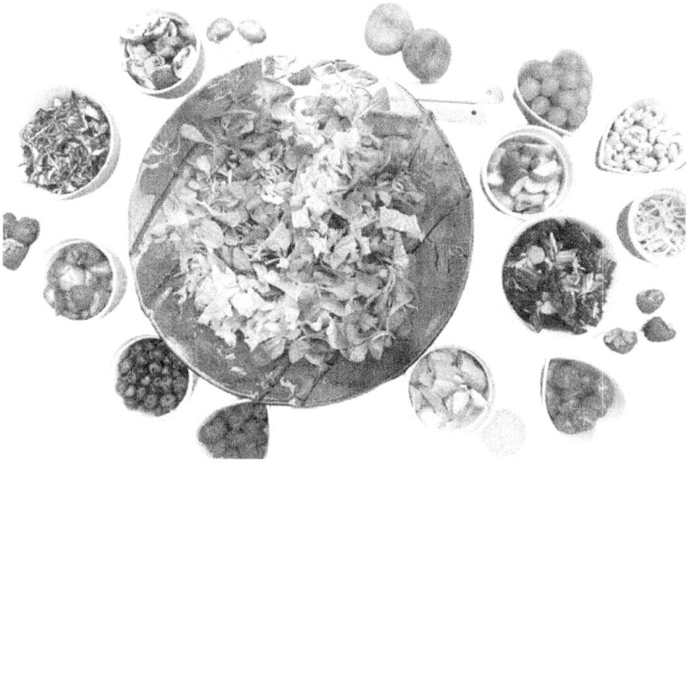

INTRODUCTION

Brief Advice for newly diagnosed

For someone freshly recognized with diabetes, it is vital to adopt a wholesome lifestyle. Start by focusing on a balanced diet with masses of greens, protein and entire grains. Find a carbohydrate supply and conclude that complex carbohydrates are in all likelihood higher than simple sugars. Regular exercise, inclusive of brisk walking or swimming, enables control of blood sugar problems and promotes general well-being. Flash returned, thickness is fundamental. Regular blood sugar tests and medical intake are vital.

Seek assistance from health experts and the Diabetes Network. Educate yourself about your illness, and do not be discouraged via your shortcomings. Diabetes surgical procedure is a adventure; Simple and wholesome adjustments in food plan, workout and voice care can result in a more healthy and happier lifestyles

Understanding Diabetes: A Brief Overview

Diabetes, a chronic medical disorder impacting millions worldwide, is a complicated interplay of elements that compromise the body's capacity to manage blood sugar levels correctly. It's necessary to dive into the complexities of this ailment to comprehend the relevance of nutrition and exercise in its management. In this comprehensive examination, we will uncover the secrets of diabetes, shining light on its forms, origins, symptoms, and then dig into the vital role that food and exercise play in minimizing its impact.

Types of Diabetes

Diabetes is not a one-size-fits-all condition; it appears in different forms. The two most frequent varieties are Type 1 and Type 2 diabetes.

1.Type 1 Diabetes: This autoimmune illness generally appears in childhood or early adulthood. In Type 1 diabetes, the immune system erroneously assaults and kills the insulin-producing beta cells in the pancreas. As a result, the body lacks insulin, a hormone necessary for controlling blood sugar. Individuals with Type 1 diabetes rely on insulin injections or insulin pumps to maintain their blood sugar levels.

2. Type 2 Diabetes: Type 2 diabetes is commonly related with lifestyle factors such as poor nutrition, sedentary activity, and obesity. In this kind, the body either does not generate enough insulin or grows resistant to its effects. Initially, lifestyle adjustments and oral drugs may be used to control Type 2 diabetes, but some persons may eventually require insulin.

There are other less prevalent kinds of diabetes, such as gestational diabetes (which arises during pregnancy) and monogenic diabetes (caused by a single gene mutation). However, Type 1 and Type 2 diabetes account for the bulk of occurrences.

Causes and Risk Factors

Understanding the origins and risk factors of diabetes is crucial to its prevention and control.

1. Type 1 Diabetes Causes: The specific etiology of Type 1 diabetes remains unknown, however it is considered to entail genetic predisposition and environmental triggers, such as viral infections.

2. Type 2 Diabetes Causes: Lifestyle factors greatly contribute to the development of Type 2 diabetes. These include poor food choices, lack of physical activity, and obesity. Genetics also play a role, as it can run in families.

Common Symptoms

Both Type 1 and Type 2 diabetes have many symptoms, including:

- Excessive thirst and hunger
- Frequent urination - Fatigue - Blurred eyesight
- Slow-healing wounds
- Unexplained weight loss (Type 1)
- Tingling or numbness in extremities (Type 2)

However, it's vital to note that some patients with Type 2 diabetes may not display significant symptoms immediately, making regular check-ups and blood sugar monitoring crucial.

The Importance of Diet in Diabetes Management

Diet is a cornerstone of diabetes control. What you consume immediately affects your blood sugar levels, making dietary choices a key tool in regulating the disease. Here are essential dietary concerns for diabetes management:

1.Carbohydrate Management:
Carbohydrates have the most significant influence on blood sugar levels. Monitoring carbohydrate consumption and preferring complex carbs (such as whole grains, legumes, and vegetables) over simple sugars helps stabilize blood sugar.

2. Balanced Meals: Aim for balanced meals that contain lean protein sources (such poultry, fish, and tofu), healthy fats (such as avocados and almonds), and a range of colorful veggies. This helps manage blood sugar and delivers critical nutrients.

3. meal Control:Be cautious of meal sizes to prevent overconsumption of calories and carbs. Measuring meals or utilizing techniques like the plate method can help with portion management.

4. Glycemic Index: Consider the glycemic index (GI) of foods, which assesses how rapidly they elevate blood sugar. Low-GI foods like steel-cut oats and quinoa are absorbed more slowly, helping maintain consistent blood sugar levels.

5. Regular Meal Timing: Stick to a regular meal plan to minimize severe changes in blood sugar. This involves eating at predictable times and avoiding missing meals.

6. Sugar & Sweeteners: Minimize added sugars and opt for natural sweeteners like stevia or tiny amounts of honey or maple syrup as needed.

7. Fiber-Rich meals: Incorporate high-fiber meals including fruits, vegetables, and whole grains into your diet. Fiber reduces the absorption of sugar and enhances intestinal health.

8. Alcohol and Sugary Beverages: Limit alcohol consumption, as it might alter blood sugar levels. Avoid sugary beverages like soda, which can trigger fast blood sugar rises.

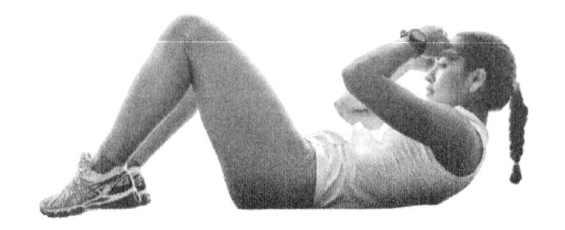

The Role of Exercise in Diabetes Management

Exercise is a formidable ally in diabetes care, having a plethora of advantages for both Type 1 and Type 2 diabetes patients. Here's why it's so essential:

1. Improved Insulin Sensitivity:
Exercise boosts the body's capacity to utilize insulin efficiently, decreasing blood sugar levels. This impact can linger for hours or even days following a workout.

2. Weight Management: Regular physical activity helps with weight reduction and weight control, a critical part of managing Type 2 diabetes, where excess body weight can contribute to insulin resistance.

3. Blood Sugar Control: Exercise helps reduce blood sugar levels directly by boosting glucose absorption by muscles. It also decreases insulin resistance, allowing cells to utilize insulin more efficiently.

4. Cardiovascular Health: Diabetes raises the risk of heart disease. Exercise promotes cardiovascular health by lowering the risk factors linked with heart disease, such as high blood pressure and cholesterol levels.

5. **Stress Reduction**:Managing stress is vital for diabetes treatment, since stress can alter blood sugar levels.

Exercise is a powerful stress reliever, increasing mental well-being.

6. Muscle Strength and

Flexibility:Building muscle via resistance exercise helps with blood sugar regulation and general physical function.

Creating an Effective Exercise Routine

Creating a tailored fitness plan is vital. Consider these tips:

1.Consult Your Healthcare Team: Talk to your healthcare professional before starting any fitness program, especially if you have underlying health conditions.

2. Choose Activities You Enjoy: Select activities you like to boost adherence. Options include walking, swimming, cycling, dancing, and yoga.

3. Aim for Consistency: Consistency is crucial. Gradually work up to at least 150 minutes of moderate-intensity aerobic activity each week, divided over at least three days.

4. Include Strength Training: Incorporate strength training activities two to three times a week, targeting key muscle groups.

5. Stay Hydrated:Proper hydration is vital, especially during activity, to minimize changes in blood sugar levels.

6. Monitor Blood Sugar: Check your blood sugar before and after exercise to understand its influence on your levels.

7. Be Prepared:Always carry a supply of fast-acting carbohydrates, like glucose tablets or juice, in case of low blood sugar (hypoglycemia) during activity.

The Synergy of Diet and Exercise

While food and exercise are important weapons separately, their interaction is much more potent.
When together, they offer comprehensive diabetes control benefits:

1.Better Blood Sugar Control:
Together, diet and exercise help maintain stable blood sugar levels, minimizing the risk of harmful spikes and crashes.

2. Weight control: This combination assists in obtaining and maintaining a healthy weight, vital for Type 2 diabetes control.

3. Reduced Medication Dependency: Many persons with Type 2 diabetes can minimize or even eliminate the requirement for medication with diet and exercise alone.

4. Cardiovascular Health: The combined impact of a good diet and regular exercise considerably improves cardiovascular health, lowering the risk of heart disease, a major consequence of diabetes.

5. Enhanced Insulin Sensitivity: When you eat correctly and exercise consistently, your cells become more receptive to insulin, making it easier for your body to control blood sugar levels.

6. Improved Overall Well-Being: Managing diabetes with nutrition and exercise isn't only about numbers on a glucose meter. It's about feeling better in your daily life, with greater energy, lower stress, and improved mood.

7. Long-Term Diabetes Management: Diet and exercise offer sustainable, long-term options for treating diabetes. They enable you to take charge of your health and lessen the need for pharmaceuticals.

Challenges and Considerations
Managing diabetes with food and exercise may offer certain obstacles, and

it's necessary to address them proactively:

1. Personalization: Diabetes is a very personalized disorder. What works for one individual may not work for another. It's vital to personalize your food and exercise regimen to your particular needs and tastes.

2. Consistency: Staying consistent with dietary choices and workout habits can be tough. Building a support network of healthcare professionals, family, and friends can help you remain on course.

3. testing: Regular blood sugar testing is necessary to understand how diet and activity affect your levels. This data can influence revisions to your plan.

4. Medical Guidance: Always work with your healthcare team, including a registered dietitian and an exercise specialist, to establish a specific strategy that corresponds with your diabetes control objectives.

5. Emotional Well-Being: Managing diabetes may be emotionally stressful. It's crucial to treat stress, anxiety, and sadness, which might impair your ability to adhere to a healthy lifestyle.

Additionally the area of diabetes control, food and exercise are not simply advice; they are effective prescriptions for a healthy life. Through conscious food choices and frequent physical exercise, persons with diabetes may greatly improve their blood sugar management, minimize the risk of complications, and boost their general well-being.

Understanding the nuances of diabetes, including its forms, causes, and symptoms, establishes the foundation for efficient care. Equipped with this knowledge, individuals may make educated judgments about their eating habits and exercise routines, working in harmony to maintain blood sugar levels steady.

While problems may emerge, the interplay of food and exercise offers a road to sustained diabetes treatment. It encourages individuals to take charge of their health, eliminate prescription reliance, and have a better quality of life. As we continue to expand our understanding of diabetes and perfect our approaches to its care, the future offers hope for even more successful solutions in the battle against this ubiquitous and problematic ailment.

Chapter one :

Diabetes-Friendly Breakfasts

Breakfast is commonly seen as the main meal of the day, and for individuals dealing with diabetes, it is essential in maintaining balanced blood sugar levels throughout the day. In this chapter, we will explore diabetes-friendly breakfast choices which not only taste delightful but also provide lasting energy and help control blood sugar levels.

1. Revitalizing Oatmeal Joy

Oatmeal is a great way to start a day off right. It's a delicious, nutritious and energizing food that provides the body with essential vitamins and minerals and helps to keep you healthy.

Oats are also naturally high in fiber which helps to aid in digestive health and keep you feeling fuller longer. Furthermore, oatmeal can be made in so many delicious ways. From basic overnight oats to oatmeal smoothies and oatmeal pancakes, the possibilities are endless. One of my favorite oatmeal recipes is the Energizing Oatmeal Delight.

This delightful dish is made with warm oats, fresh fruit and honey. It's the perfect combination of flavors that will leave you feeling energized and ready to tackle the day. The best part is, the ingredients are incredibly simple and easy to find.

All you have to do is gather the necessary items, mix them together, and you've got yourself a tasty and nutritious breakfast.

1. Reinvigorating Oatmeal Satisfaction
Oatmeal is a brilliant means of beginning the day off good. It's a yummy, nourishing, and reinvigorating food that furnishes the body with essential nutrients and encourages wellbeing. Oats are likewise coarse in fiber which helps to encourage digestive wellness and keeps you feeling full for longer. Additionally, oatmeal can be made in such a significant number of delightful ways.

From fundamental overnight oats to oatmeal beverages and oatmeal flapjacks, the potential outcomes are perpetual. One of my preferred oatmeal plans is the Reinvigorating Oatmeal Satisfaction.

This captivating dish is made with warm oats, new natural product and nectar. It's the ideal mix of flavors that will leave you feeling reinvigorated and prepared to tackle the day. The best part is, the fixings are unimaginably straightforward and anything but difficult to discover. All you need to do is gather the fundamental things, join them together, and you've got yourself a delectable and nutritious breakfast.

Oatmeal is a breakfast staple that is taken to a whole new level in this diabetes-friendly variation. It's not just about the oats; the toppings and the manner of preparation are carefully selected to make it the optimal breakfast selection for individuals with diabetes.

The dish requires the following components: half a cup of rolled oats, with whole-grain options for more fiber; one tablespoon of chia seeds; a quarter cup of unsweetened almond milk or an appropriate alternative; a half teaspoon of cinnamon; a handful of fresh berries such as strawberries, blueberries or raspberries; one tablespoon of chopped nuts like almonds or walnuts;

and one teaspoon of either honey or sugar-free sweetener (optional).

 Combine the oats, chia seeds, almond milk and cinnamon in a saucepan and place it over medium heat. Stir occasionally until the oats become soft and the mixture becomes thick (which usually takes around 5-7 minutes). Once the oats are cooked, scoop them into a bowl and garnish with fresh berries, chopped almonds and a drizzle of honey or your favorite sweetener (opting out is ok, too!).

 A delicious Scrambled Tofu Breakfast Burrito is easy to make at home. Begin by sautéing onions and bell peppers in olive oil until they are softened.

Then, add diced tofu and allow it to cook until lightly browned. Next, season the tofu with garlic powder, smoked paprika, and chili powder for a unique and flavorful experience. Lastly, add cooked black beans and fluff the mixture with a wooden spoon or spatula. Now it is time to assemble the burrito. Soften a whole wheat tortilla in a skillet, add a spoonful of Daiya vegan cheese, and then fill the tortilla with the burrito filling. Gently roll the burrito and top it with salsa and avocado for an extra kick of flavor. Enjoy this protein-packed breakfast.

For individuals who enjoy a savory morning repast,

This Scrambled Tofu Breakfast Burrito presents an appetizing option that furnishes plant protein and zesty flavor.

Ingredients:
- Half a cup of mashed firm tofu
- A quarter cup of diced bell peppers
- A quarter cup of sliced onions
- A quarter cup of spinach leaves
- A quarter teaspoon of turmeric (for color and flavor)
- Salt and pepper to taste
- Whole-grain tortilla or wrap

Heat a non-stick pan, then lightly sauté the diced onions and bell peppers. Once they have softened, add in the crumbled tofu, together with the turmeric, a pinch of salt, and pepper.

Cook all the elements until the tofu has been sufficiently cooked and has absorbed the flavors (approximately 3-5 minutes). When ready, add the spinach leaves and let them wilt for an additional minute. Afterwards, warm the tortilla or wrap, then spoon the scrambled tofu mixture into it. Lastly, wrap it up like a burrito and enjoy.

3.Increasing Energy Level with Green Smoothie

One of the easiest and most effective ways to increase one's energy level is by consuming a green smoothie. Green smoothies are packed with fresh, nutrient-dense ingredients that have an abundance of beneficial qualities.

Consuming a green smoothie gives an energy boost as well as providing essential nutrients and minerals that are necessary for a healthy lifestyle. The combination of fresh greens, fruits, and nuts is highly effective at helping to maintain vitality and promoting an energetic attitude.

Green smoothies are a great option as they are easy to prepare and can provide an immense increase in energy. The ingredients used to make a green smoothie vary, but they typically include leafy green vegetables like spinach and kale, as well as various fruits and seeds for added flavor and nutrition. Adding nuts like almonds and walnuts provides significant amounts of protein, as well as healthy fats to further support energy levels. The result is a delicious and nutritious beverage that is capable of giving an incredible boost of energy to the body.

Moreover, green smoothies can help to improve digestion and can even aid in weight loss due to its high fiber content. This in turn can provide a more sustained level of energy throughout the day. The vitamins, minerals, and antioxidants found in green smoothies also promote immunity and can help protect against disease. All of these benefits make green smoothies an excellent choice for anyone looking to increase their energy level.

Also green smoothies are an excellent way to boost energy levels while still providing important nutrients and minerals. This combination of fresh ingredients works together to create a healthful and flavorful beverage that can help improve digestion while boosting energy and protecting against disease. With its high fiber content and natural sources of vitamins and minerals, green smoothies are an ideal choice for any person looking to increase their energy and maintain overall health and vitality.
 Smoothies are a convenient and handy breakfast option for hurried mornings. This Green Smoothie Increase is packed with nutrients and can help start your day in a diabetes-friendly manner.

Ingredients:
- 1 cup of tender spinach leaves
- 1/2 fully ripe banana
- 1/4 cup of plain Greek yogurt
- 1/2 cup of unsweetened almond milk (or any alternate milk of your preference)
- 1 tablespoon of chia seeds
- Several ice cubes (optional for additional texture)

Instruction

Position the spinach, banana, Greek yogurt, almond milk, and chia seeds in a blender.
If you want a denser consistency, include a number of ice cubes.
Mix together until a homogenous

substance has been achieved, modifying the texture with additional almond milk as needed.

Transfer the green smoothie to a glass and enjoy.

These breakfast options are delectable as well as engineered to maintain your blood sugar on an even keel. They are composed of a mixture of carbohydrates, dietary fiber, protein, and heart-healthy fats, which is essential for the regulation of diabetes. Variety these recipes according to your gustatory wants while carefully monitoring portion sizes in order to ensure balanced control of your glucose levels for the duration of the day.

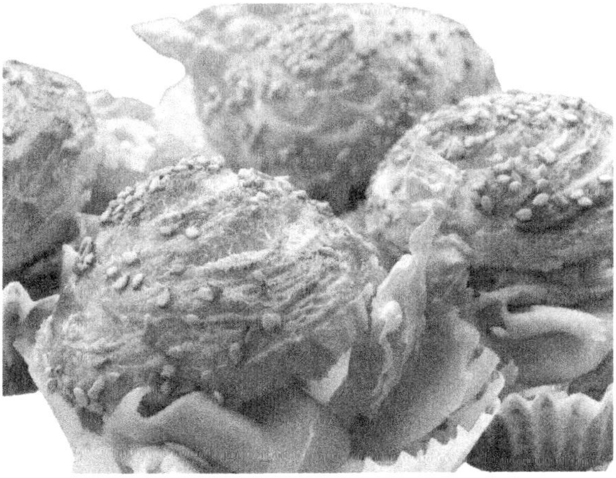

Chapter Two

Savory Lunch Creations

Lunchtime is a great chance to nourish your frame with a delicious and balanced dish that can help keep your blood sugar regulated all day long. In this article, we will discuss three yummy and diabetes-compatible lunch options that are both nutritional and packed with flavor.

 1. A flavorful Grilled Chicken and Vegetable Wrap is a great way to enjoy a delicious and nutritious meal. This wrap utilizes ingredients such as grilled

chicken breast, an assortment of vegetables, and a wrap of your choice all rolled up into one. The grilled chicken provides a savory punch while the vegetables provide crunchy texture and a

healthy component. Whether you are looking for a quick lunch or a tasty dinner, this wrap is sure to hit the spot!

This scrumptious Grilled Chicken and Veggie Wrap brings together nutritional protein and a medley of richly-hued vegetables in a convenient and handy package. It's a great selection for a full midday repast.

Ingredients:
- 4 oz of boneless, skinless chicken breast
- A whole-grain wrap
- Half a cup of assorted bell peppers, sliced
- Half a cup of zucchini, sliced
- A quarter cup of red onions, chopped
- A tablespoon of olive oil
- A teaspoon of herbs and spices of your

choice (e.g. garlic powder, paprika, or oregano)
- A pinch of salt and pepper
- Optional toppings: lettuce, tomatoes, and a light vinaigrette dressing.

Instructions:
1. Season the chicken breast with a selection of herbs and spices, salt, and pepper.
2. Heat a grill or stovetop grill pan over a medium-high flame and cook the chicken until it reaches an internal temperature of 165°F (74°C) and is no longer pink in the center (usually approximately 6-8 minutes each side).
3. While the chicken is cooking, sauté the mixed bell peppers, zucchini, and red

onion in olive oil until they are tender and lightly caramelized.

4. Heat the whole-grain tortilla or wrap.

5. Assemble your wrap by positioning the grilled chicken and sautéed vegetables on the tortilla, then add extra toppings such as lettuce and tomato, optionally.

6. Fold up the wrap and secure it with toothpicks if needed. You can also season with a mild vinaigrette dressing for added flavor.

 A delectable Quinoa and Black Bean Salad can be prepared for a tasty, wholesome meal. The ingredients are simple and easily accessible; quinoa, black beans, cilantro, lime, onion, and garlic.

The flavors are vibrant and the colors of the mix are contrasting and visually-appealing.

To begin, start by toasting the quinoa. Heat one tablespoon of oil on the stove in a medium-sized pot, then add the quinoa. Stir its grains on low heat until they become a light golden-brown. This process should take a few minutes before adding two cups of water. Bring the mixture to a boil, lower the heat and let it simmer for 15 minutes or until the quinoa appears fluffy.

The black beans should be cooked next. Put two tablespoons of oil in a separate pot and set to medium heat. Try to avoid burning the garlic, lime, and onion by thoroughly stirring them in for about a minute. Then add the beans, one teaspoon of cumin, and salt and pepper to taste. Let the mixture simmer until the beans become soft, about 10 minutes.

Once both components are ready, mix them together. Gently stir in the cilantro and the juice of one freshly-squeezed lime before allowing the salad to cool down a bit. An accompanying vinaigrette could be prepared if desired, using a simple combination of oil, vinegar, and essential seasonings.

This Quinoa and Black Bean Salad is an extremely flavorful dish that can offer numerous health benefits. The quinoa is high in protein, an important source of energy, and essential fatty acids.

The black beans are filled with beneficial fiber, vitamins, and minerals. Combined, these ingredients can create a beautiful and nutritious meal.

Salads can be immensely rewarding, and this Quinoa and Black Bean creation is no exception. Jampacked with vegetable-based protein and fiber, it's a gratifying and diabetes-friendly midday meal.

Ingredients:
- 1 cup of cooked quinoa (allowed to cool)
- 1 cup of canned black beans (washed and strained)
- 1/2 cup of cherry tomatoes (divided into halves)

- 1/4 cup of red onion (minced)
- 1/4 cup of fresh cilantro (minced)
- 1/4 cup of lime juice
- 2 teaspoons of olive oil
- 1 teaspoon of ground cumin
- A pinch of salt and pepper to taste
- Optional toppings: slices of avocado or bell peppers (sliced)

In a substantial bowl, commingle the cooked quinoa, black beans, cherry tomatoes, red onion, and cilantro.
In an individual small bowl, combine together the lime juice, olive oil, powdered cumin, salt, and pepper. Pour the dressing over the quinoa amalgamation and stir until all is fully covered.

Include different toppings such as avocado slices or chopped bell peppers for added savor and texture.

Serve the salad cooled or at ambient temperature.

Mediterranean-filled Peppers are an immensely delicious dish. Cooked in an aromatic blend of onion, garlic, herbs, and tomatoes, the peppers are stuffed with a mixture of rice, beef, and subtly seasoned vegetables. The flavourful filling and the sweet, succulent peppers bake together, creating a splendid mouth-watering meal. To top it off, a sprinkle of cheese is generously added before the peppers are finally placed in the oven and cooked until the cheese is lightly golden.

Mediterranean-filled Peppers are a delectable treat that are sure to please and not disappoint.

 Stuffed peppers offer an attractive and scrumptious lunch option. These Mediterranean Stuffed Peppers contain an appetizing combination of lean ground turkey and fragrant spices.

Ingredients:
- 2 large bell peppers (of any hue)
- 1/2 pound (around 227 grams) of lean ground turkey
- 1/2 cup of ready-made brown rice
- 1/4 cup of diced tomatoes (in jars or fresh)
- 1/4 cup of diced cucumber

- 2 teaspoons of finely diced fresh mint
- 1 tablespoon of olive oil
- 1 teaspoon of ground cumin
- Salt and pepper to season

Preheat the oven to 375°F (190°C). Subsequently, take the bell peppers and slice the tops off them, discarding the internal seeds and membranes. In a pan, warm up some olive oil, adding in the mince until it no longer retains its pink color, breaking it up through the cooking process. Once that is done, incorporate the previously cooked brown rice, diced tomatoes, diced cucumber, shreds of fresh mint, ground cumin, salt and pepper. Stir the ingredients for a few minutes to allow the flavors to combine.

Subsequently, spoon the mixture into the hollow peppers and place them in a baking dish covered with aluminum foil. Bake for 25-30 minutes until they become soft. Finally, serve the Mediterranean Stuffed Peppers piping hot, with extra mint if desired.

  These delectable lunch-time dishes are cooked to aid those with diabetes in keeping their blood sugar levels stable. Bursting with important nutrients, soluble fiber, and lean proteins, they constitute exemplary substitutes for a nutritious and wholesome midday snack. You are free to adjust these recipes to suit your individual tastes, being conscious to adhere to portion sizes for effective diabetes control.

Chapter Three:

Delectable Dinners

Dinner is an opportunity to enjoy succulent and gratifying feasts while regulating glucose concentrations. This section will overview three exquisite meal options wholly planned for diabetes control, containing exceptional flavors and nutritionally sound components.

1. Prepared Salmon with Lemon-Dill Sauce

Salmon is a popular and delicious seafood dish that has become an increasingly popular choice for dinner.

With the addition of Lemon-Dill Sauce, an easy but flavorful combination of flavors, this dish is sure to please. The rich, buttery texture of the fish paired with the zing of the lemon-dill sauce creates a delightful contrast.

To begin, preheat your oven to 375 F. Next, rinse your salmon filets and pat dry. Sprinkle with salt and pepper on both sides and place on a lightly greased pan. Bake for 10 to 12 minutes, or until the salmon's interior reaches 125 F, on an instant read thermometer.
While the salmon is baking, you can begin to make the sauce. In a small bowl, combine two tablespoons of freshly

squeezed lemon juice, two tablespoons of butter (melted), a teaspoon of dill

weed, and a pinch of salt. Whisk together and set aside.

When the salmon is done, remove from the oven and top with the lemon-dill sauce. Enjoy immediately. This salmon and lemon-dill sauce dish offers a fantastic combination of flavors that is sure to please.

Salmon is a savory treat as well as an excellent source of omega-3 fatty acids, which provide multiple wellness benefits, including assisting with regulation of diabetes.

Ingredients:
- Two salmon filets (6-8 oz each)
- Half a lemon, thinly sliced
- Two cloves of garlic, minced
- A tablespoon of freshly chopped dill
- A tablespoon of olive oil
- Salt and pepper, to taste
- Lemon-Dill Sauce (see directions below)

A delicious and light Lemon-Dill Sauce can easily be prepared by combining together a quarter cup of plain Greek yogurt, one tablespoon of lemon juice, and one teaspoon of freshly chopped dill. Add salt and pepper to taste to give this simple recipe the flavor it deserves.

1. Set your oven to 375°F (190°C).
2. Put each salmon filet on a sheet of aluminum foil big enough to cocoon it.
3. Douse the salmon with olive oil, then sprinkle with minced garlic, freshly-cut dill, salt, and pepper.
4. Layer each filet with lemon wedges.
5. Bundle the foil around the salmon to make a package, folding the sides.

6. Roast the salmon in the preheated oven for 15-20 minutes, or until it easily breaks apart with a fork.
7. While the salmon is baking, formulate the Lemon-Dill Sauce by whisking together the Greek yogurt, lemon juice, freshly-cut dill, salt, and pepper.
8. Serve the cooked salmon with a sprinkle of the Lemon-Dill Sauce.

2. Zucchini Spirals with Pesto
This delectable dish, crafted with zucchini noodles and a pleasing pesto, is sure to be a hit with family and friends alike. First, start by spiralizing your zucchini, which allows you to make long, slender strands resembling traditional noodles.

Once complete, grab a large skillet and begin to sauté the veggie noodles in a bit of olive oil, stirring occasionally, for around three minutes or until the spirals have achieved desired tenderness.

Next, it's time to assemble the entree. In the same pan, place the zucchini strands and pesto of choice into the skillet and allow to heat on low for about five minutes. As you near the end of your cooking time, be sure to taste test for seasoning and adjust as necessary.

Lastly, heap the flavorful fare onto a plate and enjoy!

This carb-free alternative to traditional pasta uses zucchini noodles, otherwise known as "zoodles," as its foundation.

Coupled with freshly-made pesto, it is a delicious and satisfactory dinner option.

Ingredients:
- 2 medium zucchinis
- 1 cup fresh basil foliage
- 1/4 cup grated Parmigiano-Reggiano
- 2 garlic cloves
- 1/4 cup pinoli
- 1/4 cup olive essenze
- Salt and pepper to individual preference
- Optional garnishes: cherry tomatoes, roasted red peppers, or sliced grilled chicken breast

Instructions:
1. Utilize a spiralizer or vegetable peeler to fashion zucchini noodles from the zucchinis.

2. Combine the basil leaves, grated Parmesan, garlic, and pine nuts into a food processor.
3. Whilst the food processor is running, carefully add the olive oil until a consistent composition is accomplished. Sprinkle salt and pepper to personal preference.
4. Blend the zucchini noodles with the pesto until they are wholly covered.
5. If desired, garnish with cherry tomatoes, roasted red peppers, or grilled chicken breast pieces to contribute flavor and protein.

 Spicy Chickpea Curry is a delectable and savory dish that packs a punch. It's full of flavor and is easy to make, making it a perfect weeknight meal.

This hearty vegan stew is loaded with nutritious ingredients such as chickpeas, tomatoes, and garlic, and it's spiced to perfection with a blend of flavorful spices. The distinct combination of flavors provides a comforting and scrumptious meal that everyone will love.

First, sauté the onion and garlic in a large pan until fragrant. Add the ground spices and allow them to fry for a couple of minutes to unlock their delicious aromas. Then, add the tomato paste and diced tomatoes to create a tomato-based sauce.
To this mixture, add the cooked chickpeas and bring the contents to a low simmer.

Allow the ingredients to simmer together for at least 30 minutes and up to an hour to give the intensity of the flavors time to fully develop. Serve the curry over steamed rice and garnish with fresh herbs and lemon wedges, if desired.

Spicy Chickpea Curry is a lip-smacking, aromatic dish that is sure to tantalize the taste buds. This scrumptious vegan stew is chock full of nutritious ingredients such as chickpeas, tomatoes, and garlic. The blend of flavorful spices creates a tasty and comforting meal in a flash. Start by frying the onion and garlic in a pan, and then add the aromatic ground spices. Following that, mix in tomato paste and diced tomatoes to form a savory sauce.

Finally, stir in the cooked chickpeas and simmer for at least thirty minutes up to an hour. Serve over steamed rice and garnish with fresh herbs and a lemon wedge for an extra zest of flavor.

Chickpeas are an excellent provider of plant-based protein and dietary fiber, making them a suitable supplement to a diabetes-friendly meal like this Spicy Chickpea Curry.

Ingredients:
- 2 cups of cooked chickpeas (canning or boiling)
- 1 onion, finely diced
- 2 cloves of garlic, minced
- 1 inch piece of ginger, grated

- 1 can (14 oz) of diced tomatoes (no extra sugar)
- 1 can (14 oz) of coco milk (light or full-fat, based upon preference)
- 1 tablespoon of olive oil
- 2 tablespoons of curry powder
- 1/2 teaspoon of cayenne pepper (adapt to preference)
- Salt and pepper to taste
- Fresh cilantro for garnishing

Heat olive oil in a pan of large proportions over a medium temperature. Incorporate the chopped onion and cook until it is objectified as transparent.
Stir in the minced garlic and the grated ginger and simmer for an additional minute until the aroam is at a notable level.

Put the curry powder, cayenne pepper, salt, and pepper into the skillet and mix everything together evenly so the onions and spices are covered.

Pour the chopped tomatoes and coconut milk into the mix and allow it to reach the boiling point.

Introduce the cooked chickpeas and then let the curry simmer for a time frame of 15 to 20 minutes in order to let all the flavours blend together.

Finally, serve the Spicy Chickpea Curry over either brown rice or quinoa and garnish with some freshly cut cilantro.

These delicious meal options are created to please your palate while promoting consistent blood sugar levels.

They emphasize the variety of items and flavors that can be a part of a diet plan that is appropriate for diabetes patients. As you savor these dishes, make sure to keep serving sizes appropriate and customize recipes according to your personal culinary preferences to make sure they meet your specific nutritional requirements.

Chapter four:

Satisfying Snacks

Nibbling can be a great part of the day, and for individuals managing diabetes, it's a chance to choose cosmetics that keep blood glucose levels stable while satisfying hunger. In this subsection, we'll investigate three appetizing and diabetes-compatible snack options that give a combination of sustenance and taste.

1. Deliciously Crunchy Trail Mix

Nutty Trail Mix is an immensely popular snack due to its convenience and. deliciousness

The mix consists of nuts, dried fruits, and sometimes some other crunchy ingredients. It is a great way to satisfy cravings and provide a quick energy boost. The variety of flavors and textures packs a flavor-punch that caters to different tastes and desires. Trail Mix is most commonly enjoyed as a snacking food; however, it can also add a much-needed nutritional boost to meals. Deliciously Crunchy Trail Mix is an immensely favored snack due to its practicality and heavenly taste. The mixture is comprised of nuts, dried fruits, and occasionally other crunchy components. It is an ideal way to slay hunger pangs and supply a quick increase in energy.

The assortment of flavors and textures delivers a flavor-barrage that caters to many different palates and hankerings. Trail Mix is often consumed as a munching food; however, it can also bestow a much-needed nutritive enhancement to dinners.

Trail mix is an in-demand treat, and when constructed with diabetes maintenance in mind, it can be a nourishing and vigor-enhancing substitute.

Ingredients:
- 1/4 cup of almonds (unsalted)
- 1/4 cup of walnuts (unsalted)
- 1/4 cup of pumpkin seeds

- 1/4 cup of unsweetened dried cranberries
- 1/4 cup of dark chocolate chips (70% cocoa at least)
- 1/4 teaspoon of cinnamon (optional)

Combine the almonds, walnuts, pumpkin seeds, dried cranberries, and dark chocolate chips in a bowl. If desired, season the blend with some cinnamon for enhanced flavor. Mix all components together until thoroughly blended. Distribute the nutty trail mix into individual servings in order to make portion control easy.

This delectable combo of nuts, seeds, dried cranberries, and dark chocolate gives you a burst of energy and provides essential heart-healthy fats. It's simple to pull together, satisfyingly sweet, and perfect for those occasions when you need an extra boost!

2. Roasted Vegetable Hummus Dipping Sauce

Hummus is one of the most beloved dips in the world. It's easy to make, which makes it popular amongst home cooks, and it's full of tasty and nutritious ingredients. One way to spice up the classic hummus recipe is to roast vegetables and mix them in. Roasting makes the vegetables sweeter and brings out complex flavors that add depth to the dip. The vegetables can be mixed with store-bought or homemade hummus and then served as a delicious and healthy snack to enjoy with friends and family.

Hummus is a wholesome and versatile dip that pairs perfectly with a variety of vegetables. This Roasted Veggie Hummus Dip offers a sumptuous mix of flavors and textures.

Ingredients:
- A selection of unprocessed vegetables (e.g. carrot batons, cucumber discs, bell pepper ribbons)
- One cup of your preferred hummus (from a shop or home-made)

1. Preheat your oven to 400°F (200°C).

2. Combine the assorted uncooked vegetables in a little olive oil, salt, and pepper.
3. Place the veggies onto a baking tray and cook them in the preheated oven for approximately 15-20 minutes or until they have softened and taken on a light brown shade.
4. Allow the roasted veggies to cool to normal temperature.
5. Serve them with a dish of hummus to dip in.

 Cooking the vegetables brings out a more intense flavor and brings out their natural sweetness. When combined with hummus, this snack offers dietary fiber, protein, and a delightful crunch.

A Greek Yogurt Parfait is an excellent way to get a filling, healthy breakfast. It's made up of layers of plain Greek yogurt, a crunchy granola-type topping, and fresh fruit. Depending on the ingredients used, it can also be high in protein and fiber, providing a balanced way to start the day.

A Greek Yogurt Parfait is an enticing morning meal. Constructed of tiers of nutrient-rich Greek yogurt, a crunchy, granola-style topping, and fresh fruit, this breakfast packs a powerful protein and fiber punch. Not only is it flavorful, but it's also nourishing, leaving you energized and ready to tackle the day ahead.

Greek yogurt is a fantastic source of protein and probiotics, making it a perfect basis for a diabetes-friendly parfait.

Ingredients:
- 1 cup of Greek yogurt (unsweetened)
- 1/2 cup assorted berries (for example, strawberries, blueberries, raspberries)
- 1/4 cup granola (opt for a low-in-sugar variety)
- 1 tablespoon of honey (optional)

Insert a glass or bowl, compile Greek yogurt, assorted berries and muesli. Include honey if you would like to sweeten it up a bit.
Repeat the layers depending on preference, and finally garnish with some extra berries.

This sumptuous Greek Yogurt Parfait provides a delightful fusion of richness, crunchiness, and natural succulence.

The Greek yogurt gives protein, the berries administer fiber and antioxidants, and the granola furnishes a delightful texture.

 These delectable treats are crafted to keep your energy chemistry even, while providing important nutritional value. Perfect for taming after-lunch appetite or satiating evening cravings. As with any sort of munching, measuring the amount eaten is key to successful diabetes management, hence consuming thoughtfully and in limited amounts is essential.

Chapter five

Diabetic-Friendly Desserts

Achieving your desire for sweetness while managing diabetes is attainable with appropriate dessert choices. In this article, we'll consider three scrumptious and diabetes-friendly desserts that

provide sweetness without compromising sugar level regulation.

1. Berry Euphoric Chia Custard
This sumptuous pudding is a nutritious treat that's sure to impress. The delightful combination of chia seeds and berries is a flavor that is simply delightful.

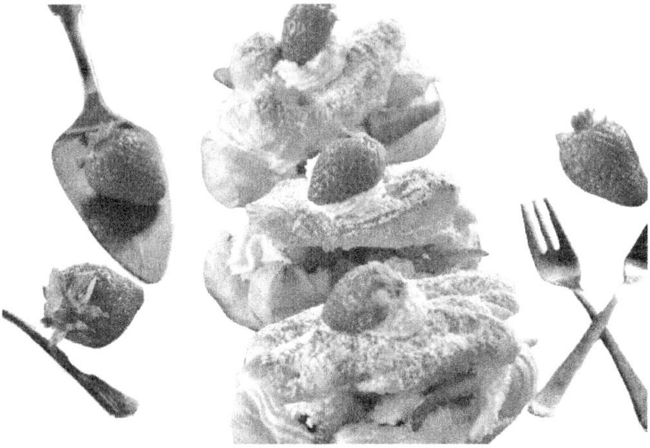

The chia seeds provide a crunchy texture, while the rich flavor of the berries gives this pudding a delectable flavor. The creamy goodness of coconut milk makes this a heavenly dessert that will leave your taste buds tingling. And the best part? This recipe is packed with nutrients, making it an ideal snack for when you are feeling peckish. The chia and berries provide a powerful mix of antioxidants, fiber and omega-3 fatty acids, so it's good for your heart, too. Enjoy this sweet treat and rest assured that you are doing your body good.

Chia pudding is a delightfully soothing treat that is crammed with dietary fiber and beneficial fatty acids.

The addition of berries supplies a delectable dose of sweetness along with powerful antioxidants.

Ingredients:
- 3 tbsps of chia seeds
- 1 cup of unsweetened almond milk (or the milk you prefer)
- 1/2 tsp of vanilla essence
- 1/2 cup of varied berries (e.g. strawberries, blueberries and raspberries)
- 1 tbsp of finely chopped nuts (e.g. almonds or walnuts)
- 1 tsp of honey or sugar-free sweetener (optional)

1. Combine the chia seeds, almond milk, and vanilla extract in a bowl and mix together thoroughly.
2. Cover the bowl and refrigerate the blend for 3 hours or longer, so that the chia seeds can absorb the liquid and become pudding-like.
3. When the pudding is ready, garnish it with a mix of berries and chopped almonds.
4. Add a dash of honey or whatever sweetener you enjoy for even more sweetness, if desired.

This creative, Berry Bliss Chia Pudding provides a sensational dessert that does not cause sudden rises in blood sugar. Abundant in fiber, chia seeds supply omega-3 fatty acids, and the sweet tones of fresh berries enrich the flavor.

2. Avocado Chocolate Mousse
Nothing could be more delectable than this sinfully delicious sweet treat. With the perfect combination of rich cocoa flavors and creamy avocado textures, this dessert is the ideal solution for any occasion. It's easy to make and only requires a few simple ingredients.

This scrumptious delight consists of cocoa, avocado, and sweetener - usually sugar or honey. Start by combining the cocoa and sweetener in a small bowl to form a thick, creamy paste. Then, in a separate bowl, mash the avocado in a fork until it becomes a smooth texture. Finally, blend the cocoa and avocado into the paste.

To finish off your mousse, you can chill and serve it with a dollop of sugar or honey. You can also top the creamy mixture with some grated or melted dark chocolate curls. This decadent creation can be enjoyed all year round and is sure to satisfy any sweet tooth.

This yummy treat is not only delicious, but also packs a hefty nutritional punch. The avocado is packed with healthy fats that provide essential fatty acids for your body. Avocado also contains vitamins

B-6 and C, fiber, magnesium, and copper, making it a very nutritious snack. The dark cocoa is also beneficial to your health and helps to improve overall cardiovascular health.

Get ready to indulge with this divine Avocado Chocolate Mousse. It's the perfect way to delight your taste buds and indulge in some guilt-free pleasure. With its irresistible flavours, it's sure to be a crowd-pleaser!

Avocado-chocolate mousse is a voluptuous and luscious delicacy that's nutritious too. Avocado grants beneficial fats and a silky texture, while cocoa powder renders an intense chocolate flavor.

Ingredients required:
- 2 fully matured avocados
- 1/4 cup of plain cocoa
- 1/4 cup of almond milk (or an alternative of your preference)
- 1/4 cup of sugar-free sweetener (i.e. erythritol or stevia)
- 1 teaspoon of vanilla essence
- A pinch of salt
- Fresh berries for decoration (optional)

Instructions:
1. Split the avocados in two, remove the cores, and scoop the interior into a blender or food processor.
2. Place the unsweetened cocoa powder, almond milk, sugar-free sweetener,

vanilla extract, and a pinch of salt in the blender.

3. Puree until a smooth and velvety consistency is reached, stirring the edges as needed for a consistent blending.

4. Divide the avocado chocolate mousse into individual dishes.

5. Refrigerate for at least an hour to attain a chilled temperature and let the flavors develop.

6. Top with fresh berries to embellish the dish before presenting.

 This Avocado Chocolate Mousse is an exquisite delicacy that combines beneficial fats and a delightful chocolate indulgence while being diabetes-friendly.

3. Cinnamon-Spiced Baked Apples offer an interesting twist on a classic comfort food. Prepared in the oven, the tart-sweet combination produces a dish that's both delectable and pleasingly aromatic. To begin, core the apples and cut into halves or wedges. Place the pieces in an oven-safe dish and sprinkle liberally with cinnamon. For an added hint of sweetness, add some sugar or honey. Bake the apples at 375°F for 20-25 minutes. Serve warm, with either a dollop of ice cream or a drizzle of caramel. Enjoy this simple yet delicious dessert that offers up authentic autumn flavors.

Baked apples serve as a comforting and healthfully sweet after-dinner treat. Cinnamon is included to grant them an extra layer of flavor, while simultaneously providing a pleasant touch of warmth, without the need to add extra sugar.

Two apples, such as Granny Smith or Honeycrisp, can be used for this recipe; a 1/2 teaspoon of ground cinnamon, 1/4 teaspoon of powdered nutmeg, 1/4 teaspoon of ground cloves, 1/4 cup of chopped nuts, such as pecans or almonds; a tablespoon of melted coconut oil (or butter if preferred), and a teaspoon of honey or a sugar-free alternative, if desired.

Before you start, preheat your oven to 375°F (190°C). Cut the apples in two and discard the cores to create a hollow for your filling. In a bowl, mix together the cinnamon, nutmeg, cloves, minced almonds, melted coconut oil (or butter), and honey or sugar-free sweetener (if desired). Place the stuffing into the prepared apples and put them on a baking tray. Cook in the oven for around 20-25 minutes or until the apples are tender and lightly browned. Serve the completed dish warm.

These Cinnamon-Infused Baked Apples present an inviting and comforting dessert without requiring additional sweeteners.

The invigorating blend of the apples, spiced aromatically and punctuated with toasty nuts, creates a titillating and satisfying dish perfect for diabetes sufferers.

Chapter six

Exercise Routines

Physical activity is a beneficial approach for individuals who are monitoring diabetes. In this section, we will explore the various aspects of exercising that can benefit those with diabetes, from the merits of habitual physical activity to particular kinds of workouts that can help

moderate blood glucose and decrease tension.

1. Regular exercise offers numerous advantages for those affected by diabetes. It increases one's capacity to manage blood sugar levels, promotes weight loss, and fortifies the body's capability to utilize insulin. Exercise facilitates an improvement in overall health in diabetics by enhancing cardiovascular fitness, leading to reduced risk of heart diseases. Additionally, it reduces stress and depression, boosts energy levels, promotes better sleep, strengthens the bones, and encourages social well-being. To receive the greatest health benefits,

it's important to aim for engaging in at least 150 minutes of exercise each week. By doing so, it can help prevent or manage type 2 diabetes and can improve the overall health of those already afflicted with the disease.

Regular exercise offers a variety of benefits for those with diabetes: Exercise assists with maintaining blood sugar levels by enabling increased glucose uptake by the muscles, decreasing resistance to insulin, and improving receptiveness to the hormone.

Maintaining a healthy weight is a fundamental element in managing diabetes, especially for those with Type 2 diabetes, as extra weight can result in insulin resistance.

The practice of exercise can help in lessening the prospects of coronary heart disease, an effect of diabetes in many cases. Physically active individuals are likely to have lower blood pressure, lower cholesterol, and heightened cardiovascular health.

The effective management of stress is of paramount importance for proper diabetes care, as it can notably affect blood sugar levels. Exercise is a powerful way to reduce tension and heighten mental health.

Improved Sleep:Regular exercise can lead to increased sleep quality, which is vital for general health and diabetes control.

Cardiac exercises are an important component of overall fitness. When done correctly, they can help improve cardiovascular health and endurance. Cardiovascular exercises involve activities like running, biking, swimming, and jumping rope that stimulate the heart and lungs. During exercise, the heart pumps faster, the body produces more oxygen, and breathing becomes deeper and more regular. This helps to increase overall cardiovascular fitness and reduce the risk of disease. Additionally, these activities can help to burn calories and improve one's overall physical condition.

Cardiovascular workouts are proven to have a plethora of health benefits. Working out improves the circulation of blood and oxygen to the heart and other organs. This, in turn, reduces stress on the cardiovascular system, and helps to prevent the development of many conditions such as heart disease, high blood pressure and stroke. Additionally, engaging in cardiovascular exercise increases endorphin levels, putting an individual in a better state of mind.
Regular exercise also reduces the risk of developing diabetes and certain types of cancer.
Ultimately, cardiovascular workouts are essential for maintaining mental and physical health.

In order to reap the full benefits, adequate time should be devoted to engaging in such activities. Developing a regular routine can improve overall fitness and well-being, reduce the risk of disease, and foster a feeling of contentment and satisfaction. Therefore, cardio exercises should be a vital component of any life plan.

Cardiovascular workouts, often referred to as aerobic activities, are beneficial for treating diabetes, as they help bring down blood sugar levels and promote heart health. The following are just a few of the options available for cardiovascular exercise:

Engaging in Striding:Striding is an attainable and efficient aerobic exercise. Target at least 150 minutes of swift walking every week, spread out over a minimum of three days.

 riding:Whether on a stationary bike or outside, riding gives a low-impact cardiovascular workout.
Swimming: Engaging in aquatic exercise is a great way to keep the body healthy and maintain champion cardiovascular health. It is a total-body workout that is easy on the joints. Additionally, it can help boost stamina and overall health.
 For those who enjoy the pleasure of running, it is an ideal method to spike

one's pulse. Nonetheless, commencement should take place cautiously, considering the terrain and properly fitted footwear to protect your joints.

Strength training is an effective way to lower your blood sugar levels. Research has shown that engaging in regular resistance exercise can help manage your body's response to the sugar levels in your bloodstream. Through this type of exercise, your body strengthens its muscles and improves its overall strength. This can improve your ability to regulate your blood sugar levels and reduce the need to take medications for diabetes or other conditions related to fluctuating blood sugar levels.

With strength training, your body gets better at using glucose, which is a type of sugar found in your bloodstream.

Regular exercise helps to ensure that this glucose is used more efficiently by the body's cells.

This can help to reduce your risk of developing serious medical problems related to high blood sugar levels, such as heart disease and stroke.

Training with weights can also help you better manage your weight. Resistance exercise helps to increase lean muscle mass which in turn helps burn more calories. This can contribute to weight loss, which is an important factor in maintaining healthy blood sugar levels. Furthermore, added muscle mass increases your body's ability to use glucose, thus assisting in better blood sugar control.

engage in regular strength training if you're looking for an effective way to manage your blood sugar levels. Not only will this type of exercise help to improve your overall strength, but it can also result in better glucose metabolism and weight control. All of this can help to reduce the risk of serious complications from high blood sugar levels.
 Strength training, often referred to as

Resistance exercise is an essential part of a diabetes management plan. Increasing muscle mass can help to improve insulin sensitivity. The following are some popular strength training routines you can incorporate into your routine:

 A well-rounded strength training routine should include exercises for all major muscle groups, working out 2-3 times per week.
Yoga has been widely recognized as an effective way to cope with stress. Its numerous physical and psychological benefits make it a highly desirable practice for many. By performing yoga

postures and engaging in deep breathing exercises, one can significantly reduce the amount of stress they experience. This is due to the calming effects of yoga, which can help to decrease blood pressure and relax the body and mind. In addition, the practice of yoga encourages heightened awareness of the body and breath, as well as acceptance of any physical, mental, and emotional blocks that could be contributing to high levels of anxiety and stress.

Through regular practice, people can learn how to control their level of stress and improve their overall well-being. Furthermore, yoga is often recommended as part of a comprehensive lifestyle approach to stress management that incorporates healthy eating, exercise, and adequate rest. By incorporating yoga into a daily

routine, individuals can become better equipped to tackle stressors and navigate daily life more calmly and confidently.

Stress regulation is essential for mastering diabetes, as tension can spike blood sugar levels. Yoga is an ideal choice for workout and stress relief. By combining physical postures, deep breathing, and meditation, this practice encourages relaxation and increases flexibility.

Hatha Yoga: A gentle form of yoga suitable for beginners, focusing on basic postures and breathing.
Restorative Yoga is a peaceful form of yoga which utilises helpful items to support the figure in various poses, instigating a sense of calm.

Regular yoga practice can reduce stress, improve mental clarity, and positively impact blood sugar control. Including these workout regimens in your lifestyle can be very beneficial for managing diabetes. It is important to speak with your healthcare provider before launching a new exercise regimen, particularly if you have underlying health problems.

They can customize a workout plan to fit your particular needs and guarantee your safety as you strive for better blood sugar control and improved health.

Chapter seven

Meal Planning and Portion Control

Effective meal planning and quantity control are crucial factors of successful diabetes treatment. In this chapter, we will discuss helpful recommendations for balanced meal planning and tactics to help you regulate your portions to maintain stable blood sugar levels.

Tips for Balanced Meal Planning

Balanced meal planning is the basis of diabetes control. It entails picking the correct foods in the proper amounts to maintain blood sugar levels steady. Here are some recommendations to help you prepare balanced meals:

1.Choose Whole Foods:Opt for full, unprocessed foods including fruits, vegetables, whole grains, lean meats, and healthy fats. These meals are high in minerals and fiber,

which helps manage blood sugar.
2. Practice Carbohydrate Counting:Carbohydrates have the most important influence on blood sugar. Learn to measure carbs in your meals and pick complex carbohydrates with a low glycemic index (GI) to prevent abrupt increases in blood sugar.
3. Focus on Fiber: Include high-fiber foods like beans, grains, and leafy greens in your meals. Fiber slows down the digestion

and absorption of carbs, helping to balance blood sugar.

4. Incorporate Lean Proteins: Protein-rich meals including poultry, fish, tofu, and beans will help you feel full and regulate blood sugar levels. Include a source of protein in each meal.

5. Healthy Fats: Incorporate sources of healthy fats including avocados, nuts, seeds, and olive oil.

These fats can enhance insulin sensitivity and create a sensation of fullness.

6. Watch Portion Sizes: Be aware of portion amounts to avoid overeating. Measuring meals, using smaller plates, and paying attention to hunger signs can help.

7. Regular Mealtimes:Stick to a regular eating routine. Spacing meals appropriately throughout the day can help minimize

significant swings in blood sugar levels.

8. Limit Sugary Foods: Minimize the consumption of sugary snacks, sweets, and sugary beverages, as these can cause fast rises in blood sugar.

9. Hydrate:Drink plenty of water throughout the day to keep hydrated. Dehydration can influence blood sugar regulation.

10. Meal Prep:Consider meal

planning to have healthy, balanced meals easily available. This can help you make better eating choices and avoid impulsive, less nutritious decisions.

Portion Control Strategies

Portion management is vital for balancing calorie consumption and blood sugar levels. Here are some techniques to help you limit your portions effectively:

1.Use Smaller dishes

2.Choose smaller dishes and bowls to assist visibly regulate portion proportions. A smaller dish may make a decent portion look more substantial.

2. Measure meal:Use measuring cups and a kitchen scale to measure meal quantities correctly, especially for things like rice, pasta, and cereal.

3. Follow the Plate Method: Divide your plate into sections:

half for non-starchy veggies, one-quarter for lean protein, and one-quarter for carbs. This strategy helps you produce balanced meals.

4. Avoid Mindless consuming: Pay attention to what you're consuming. Avoid eating directly from a bag or container, as it might lead to overeating.
5. relish Each Bite:Eat slowly and appreciate each bite. This allows your body time to signal fullness, reducing overconsumption.

6. Practice Mindful Eating:Be conscious of hunger and fullness cues. Stop eating when you're satisfied, not excessively stuffed.

7. Use Food Labels:Read food labels to understand serving sizes and nutritional information. Pay attention to the overall carbohydrate content.

8. Plan foods: Pre-portion foods into tiny containers or packets to avoid overindulging when munching.

9. Share meals:When dining out, consider sharing meals with others to limit portion sizes and calorie consumption.

10. Practice Self-Control: Remember that portion control is a skill that can be learned over time. Be patient with yourself and make incremental improvements.

Balanced meal planning and quantity control are crucial skills for diabetes treatment.

By making intelligent decisions about the items you eat and the quantities you consume, you may better manage your blood sugar levels and preserve general health. Consult with a qualified dietitian or healthcare practitioner for specialized counseling and meal planning tactics geared to your unique requirements and objectives.

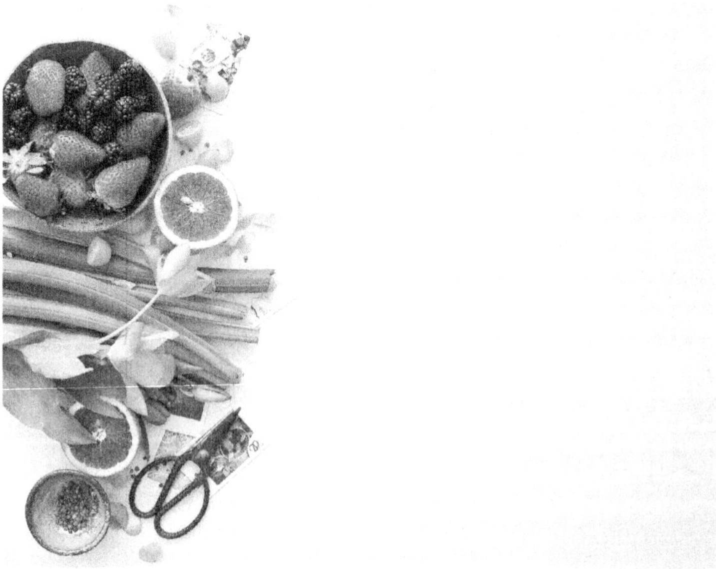

Chapter Eight:

Managing Blood Sugar

Managing blood sugar is at the heart of diabetes care. Within this thorough chapter, we will explore the pivotal aspects of observing one's glucose levels and handling hypoglycemia and hyperglycemia correctly. These techniques are of paramount importance for keeping consistent blood sugar levels and averting difficulties.

Monitoring Blood Glucose Levels
Regular surveying of blood glucose

concentrations is a vital element of diabetes management.It furnishes key insights to make considered decisions regarding medications, dietary intake, and exercise. Here's how to competently monitor your blood glucose levels:

Select a Glucose Meter: Make a judicious choice of a dependable glucose monitor that meets your requirements. A plethora of models exist - some outfitted with Bluetooth for monitoring and analyzing data.
Before conducting the test, make sure to scrub your hands with lukewarm, sudsy water to get rid of any contaminants that could adversely affect the accuracy of the outcome.

Ready the Lancet Device: Equip the lancet unit as instructed by the producer. Alter the profundity configuration to get a decent example of blood.

Employ the lancet to carefully puncture the periphery of your fingertip. Evade the central area since it may be more sensitive.

Gather a Blood Specimen: Enable a tiny droplet of blood to manifest at the punctured location. Adjoin the blood globule to the analysis slip of the glucose detector.

After a few moments, the meter will reveal your blood sugar reading. If you are tracking your information, make sure to log the results in either a diary or a smartphone app.

Over the long term, pursue your blood sugar readings to discern trends and sequences. This could help you and your healthcare provider alter your diabetes management plan as necessary.

 Your healthcare professional will recommend when and how often you should assess your blood sugar. Ordinary testing times comprise fasting (in the morning), antecedent to eating meals, following meals, and before slumber.
 Ensure that your glucose meter produces precise readings by conforming to the manufacturer's specifications. If a calibration is necessary, heed the

instructions for attaining dependable results.

Occasionally, corroborate the readings from your instrument with laboratory blood tests to ensure reliability.

Be Aware of Contexts That Modify Results. Bear in mind that various contexts such as pressure, maladies, medications, and liquor can modify blood sugar numbers. Give due consideration to these aspects when you make judgments based on the readings.

Hypoglycemia and Hyperglycemia: What to Do

Individuals with diabetes may face daunting challenges in the forms of hypoglycemia (low blood sugar) and hyperglycemia (high blood sugar). It is essential to comprehend the signs and strategies for handling such conditions for your wellbeing and security.

Hypoglycemia (Low Blood Sugar)
Hypoglycemia is a medical condition characterized by abnormally low blood sugar levels. Its symptoms may range from mild to serious, such as:

1. Test Your Blood Sugar: Check your blood sugar level to ensure that it's low. Consume Quickly-Digested Carbs: Ingest or imbibe something consisting of

quickly-digested carbs to heighten your blood sugar expeditiously. Instances include:
- 15-20 grams of dextrose pills or jelly
- 4 ounces of fruity juice or traditional soda
- 1 tablespoon of sweetener or saccharose

After consuming carbohydrates, wait for approximately 15 minutes and then measure your blood glucose level.

If your glucose concentrations remain inadequate, keep treating yourself until it registers an acceptable value (commonly more than 70 mg/dL or whatever advised by your healthcare provider).

Once your glucose level is steady, eat a small snack that contains a combination of protein and carbohydrates in order to prevent further decline.

If you find your hypoglycemia to be very severe or not able to take care of it by yourself, it is essential to get medical attention immediately. For more serious hypoglycemia, you may need a glucagon shot, which can be carried out by another person.

Hyperglycemia (High Blood Sugar)
Hyperglycemia is an ailment that occurs when an individual's blood sugar level is too high.

Common symptoms can comprise of:

1. Test Your Blood Sugar: Confirm if your blood sugar is high by testing with your glucose meter.
Be Sure To Stay Hydrated: Ingest an abundant amount of water to facilitate the elimination of surplus glucose from your anatomy and avert desiccation.

If you are taking diabetic medication, make sure you adhere to your healthcare specialist's instructions concerning adjusting your dosage in order to bring your glucose levels down.

If you struggle with Type 1 diabetes, it is essential to monitor your ketones by means of ketone test strips. Elevated levels of ketones may suggest the presence of diabetic ketoacidosis (DKA), a condition that necessitates speedy medical attention.

Assess your current meals and snacks. Contemplate if you have taken in additional carbohydrates or left out insulin injections.

Physical activity of a minimal intensity can assist in bringing down blood sugar levels. Prior to engaging in physical exercise, it is vital for those with a high blood sugar reading to seek the advice of their healthcare professional.

Reach out to your medical practitioner: If you find that your blood glucose level has stayed abnormally high in spite of your measures, get in touch with your healthcare provider for support. They may need to modify your treatment plan.

Creating a Sick-Day plan is essential if you are ill as it will help you manage your blood sugar levels. Modifying your medications and keeping consistent track of your readings are key elements to this strategy. This approach can make a big difference to your overall health and well-being during illness.

Be careful not to take too much insulin to compensate for elevated blood sugar levels, as this could cause hypoglycemia. Overcorrection is to be avoided.

If blood sugar levels are significantly high and accompanied by concerning symptoms such as confusion or nausea, it is essential to seek urgent medical care.

Maintaining healthy blood sugar levels is a laborious effort that necessitates constant awareness and comprehension. Routine observation combined with familiarity of hypoglycaemic episodes are key in regulating blood sugar levels effectively.

Chapter Nine

Additional Resources

In pursuit of handling diabetes in a successful fashion, it is essential to have access to effective resources and support structures. This section provides details of diabetic encouragement groups as well as suggested literature and webpages which can offer beneficial advice and upliftment.

Diabetes Support Groups

Living with diabetes is often difficult, yet it isn't something you have to face in solitude. Diabetes support communities offer a sense of fellowship, shared circumstances, and useful assistance.

Perceive attending a local or online
diabetic support group to bond with those

who grasp your emotions. Here's how they can lend a hand:

Emotional Assistance: Diabetes support groups offer a safe space to express your concerns and feelings. Reaching out to people who can relate to you and your struggles can be profoundly comforting.

Members habitually converse regarding counsel and procedures for handling diabetes effortlessly. You may garner insight from others' victories and tribulations.

Belonging to a preserving group can boost your determination to make healthy lifestyle choices and keep to your diabetes treatment schedule.

Friendship: It is possible to create meaningful bonds with those who share similar experiences, potentially resulting in relationships that span a lifetime.

Members may share their knowledge on the newest studies, treatments, and advances related to diabetes.

Accountability: Recognizing that others are diligently tracking their achievements may spur you to remain consistent with your diabetes care.

It is possible to find diabetic support groups in a variety of formats, such as in-person meetings, online conversation forums, and social media circles. The American Diabetes Association and similar organizations often provide resources to aid in locating a support group that is suitable for individual needs.

1. The American Diabetes Association Complete Guide to Diabetes" by American Diabetes Association
This comprehensive text discusses multiple facets of diabetes management, including diet, exercise, medication, and psychological well being. It is an invaluable source of information for both

newly diagnosed people and those who want to expand their diabetes awareness.

Think Like a Pancreas: A Handy Guide to Taking Command of Diabetes with Insulin by Gary Scheiner provides a comprehensive primer on key tactics to regulate your condition via insulin. Subjects like dosage, sugar testing, and diet preparation all get detailed attention in his guide.

The American Diabetes Association has produced a magazine entitled 'Diabetes Forecast', which aims to provide individuals affected by the condition with the latest advice and updates. This resource is written in a clear and concise manner, in order to best benefit those who use it. By subscribing to the magazine, individuals have the opportunity to receive regular updates on the latest clinical advancements and innovative approaches to managing diabetes. It is also tailored to the needs of different age groups, ensuring all readers have access to relevant information and advice, allowing them greater autonomy over their diabetes management. Furthermore, readers are kept informed of related topics, such as nutrition, exercise and psychology, helping them to live healthier and more fulfilling lives. The magazine provides readers with a comprehensive resource they can rely on to stay up to date on the most important developments in the field.

This monthly publication comprises articles, exhortations, and recipes to assist you in staying informed and inspired to handle your diabetes. It covers an extensive array of topics, from cutting edge research to life-altering stories of success.

Diabetes self-care is an often overlooked but essential part of managing the deadly illness. By taking charge of their health, individuals with diabetes can lead a more comfortable and secure life. Proper diet, regular exercise, and monitoring of blood sugar levels are all essential components of diabetes maintenance. Adhering to one's dietary plan and making sure to get regular physical activity helps to keep sugar levels in check. It is also important for diabetics to have their blood sugar tested regularly to monitor their progress and detect any potential issues. Lastly, individuals with diabetes must pay close attention to any symptoms of hypoglycemia and hyperglycemia to avoid dangerous complications. By focusing on these aspects, those with diabetes can work towards having a happier and healthier life.

The Diabetes Self-control website and periodical afford a great deal of knowledge about managing diabetes, featuring pieces on nutrition, physical activity, treatments, and advice for living well.

 The Joslin Diabetes Center website furnishes a wide range of items, comprising instructional resources, recipes, and directives for managing diabetes. In addition, they also supply online classes and access to specialist diabetes treatment.
 Diabetes Daily is an interactive web-based resource for individuals suffering from diabetes. It provides a

bevy of data, forums, and culinary options, along with a helpful cadre of individuals with diabetes. The platform opens up the knowledge and support needed to lead an empowered life.

Beyond Type 1 is an altruistic association devoted to providing aid and assistance to those coping with Type 1 diabetes. Their website hosts entries, individual accounts, and an interconnected online environment.

The Diabetes Forecast Podcast, a production of the American Diabetes Association, provides a broad selection of topics related to diabetes, including diet, exercise, psychological health, and heartening stories from the GDP community. It's an ideal approach to stay updated and motivated in one's journey.

These suggested reading materials and websites are invaluable sources of wisdom and motivation for those living with diabetes. Whether you're in search of practical counsel, emotional encouragement, or the latest research, these resources can support you on your journey to best diabetes control.

Conclusion

Embracing a Healthier Lifestyle with Diabetes

Living with diabetes presents countless difficulties, but it concurrently offers an opportunity to take control of one's well-being and incarnate a beneficial manner of life. Throughout this publication, we have scrutinized multiple facets of diabetes administration, including comprehending the disease and supervising blood glucose levels, constructing a judicious diet, exercising on a regular basis, and obtaining assistance from others.

As we come to the end of this expedition, let's take the time to recall the primary teachings and the appetizing and healthy meals that can make this lifestyle not only achicvablc but cnjoyablc.

Key Takeaways:
Gaining knowledge is invaluable: gaining insight into diabetes, its variations, and the impact it has on the body is the primary step towards sound management. Being informed allows you to make informed decisions which can only be to the benefit of yourself.
A balanced diet is the cornerstone of diabetic management. Put emphasis on nourishing, undiluted meals, portion

management, and mindful consumption. Awareness of carbohydrate counting and glycemic index can empower you to make sounder food choices.

Adopting physical activity into a day-to-day system can provide a plethora of advantages, including augmented glucose levels, weight administration, and augmented overall health. Cardio exercises, authority training, and pastimes, like yoga, are all eminently appropriate for a fitness agenda.

Regularly checking your blood sugar levels is essential for determining how your body responds to various diet plans, physical activities and medications. Make use of a glucose meter to trace your progress and adjust your diabetes management program as necessitated.

Understanding the detection and response to lows (hypoglycemia) and highs (hyperglycemia) of your blood sugar levels is important for your security. Rapid and urgent intervention can help to avoid any issues.

You're certainly not solitary on your journey. Diabetes support collectives, whether in-person or digital, afford a sense of fellowship, emotional succor, and useful direction. Hooking up with people who share your ordeals could be an inspiring occurrence.

Remain Educated: Stay abreast of the most current conclusions and progress in diabetes care. Think about looking through recommended books and navigating dependable websites to amplify your knowledge.

Delicious and Nutritious Recipes to Savor:

Throughout this book, we have presented you with a range of flavorful and beneficial dishes tailored for managing diabetes. Let's explore a few of these meals to get you motivated as you undertake your culinary adventure:

A hearty and satisfying breakfast can be achieved by stirring oats with cinnamon and garnishing the bowl with berries and nuts. A delicious cup of oats is an excellent way to kickstart your day with energy.

Mediterranean Stuffed Peppers deliver a delightful dish filled with quinoa, black beans, and other Mediterranean components. This colorful creation is both nutritious and scrumptious.

Indulge your sweet tooth with a velvety and guilt-free confection crafted from avocados and cacao powder. This delectable dessert won't cause your glucose levels to soar.

Create a delectable and nutritious snack or breakfast by layering Greek yogurt with a combination of berries and granola. Not only is this a delightful combination, but it will also keep you feeling satiated and energized.

A wholesome and invigorating chickpea stew accompanied by brown rice or quinoa is a delectable and high fiber meal choice that won't leave you let down.

6. Roasted Vegetable Hummus Dip: An appetizing and healthful snack can be crafted by blending roasted vegetables with creamy hummus, which is perfect for dipping.

Cinnamon-Spiced Baked Apples: These baked apples spiced with cinnamon and garnished with almonds offer up a delightful dessert or nibble.

These dishes give a glimpse into the appetizing and diverse options available to those with diabetes. They showcase the variety of ingredients and tastes that can be included in a diabetes-friendly diet. With a creative spirit and a commitment to making health-conscious decisions, you can enjoy a wide selection of dishes while keeping your health as a top priority.

30 Days Meal Plan to Manage Type 1 diabetes ,Type 2 Diabetes and borderline diabetes

As you persevere with diabetes, remind yourself that it's not about denial or limits; it's about making informed decisions, embracing a healthy lifestyle, and relishing the abundance of delectable dishes that might advance your health. Diabetes regulation is a perpetual undertaking, but with the proper education, sustenance, and culinary creativeness, you can live a meaningful and vigorous existence.

Understanding Diabetes Types:
Before delving into the dietary regimen, it is important to understand the distinctions between Type 1 diabetes, Type 2 diabetes, and prediabetes (also known as borderline diabetes).

Type 1 Diabetes: This is an autoimmune ailment in which the body's immune system destroys the cells in the pancreas that make insulin. People with Type 1 diabetes should take insulin by injection or a pump in order to regulate their blood sugar levels.

Type 2 Diabetes is a condition marked by a failure of the body's cells to accurately respond to insulin. Initially, the pancreas works to produce extra insulin, but eventually it may not be enough. To manage Type 2 diabetes, lifestyle adaptations including modifications to diet and exercise are essential. In some cases, medications or insulin injections may also be necessary.

Borderline Diabetes (Prediabetes): This condition results when blood sugar levels are above the norm but have not yet reached the level indicating Type 2 diabetes. It is a telltale sign that appropriate management of blood sugar is necessary to counteract the progress of Type 2 diabetes.

 A well-crafted meal plan for diabetes treatment tries to meet numerous goals: The fundamental objective is to keep blood sugar levels even over the course of the day, steering clear of dramatic peaks and troughs.
 Mealtimes should incorporate an equilibrium of carbohydrates, proteins,

and unsaturated fats. To facilitate the stabilized processing of carbohydrates, high-fiber meals are essential.

Observing the sizes of one's portions is an important factor to consider in order to avert overindulgence and control calorie consumption.

Maintaining a regular schedule of eating can be advantageous in regulating blood sugar levels. Strive for having three main meals plus some nutritious snacks between meals.

The meal plan should feature a wide range of diverse dishes and flavors to keep things interesting and to facilitate enjoyment of the eating experience.

It Sample 30-Day Meal Plan

This is a tentative 30-day meal regimen that can be tailored to the distinct needs of people with Type 1 diabetes, Type 2 diabetes, or pre-diabetes. It is crucial to seek out the advice of a qualified medical professional or trained dietician in order to customize the plan to fulfill your own individual needs and desires.

Week 1:
Day 1- Breakfast: Scrambled omelet with sautéed spinach and diced tomatoes
- Lunch: Grilled chicken mixed greens salad with vinaigrette dressing
- Snack: Greek yogurt topped with fresh berries

- Dinner: Baked salmon with roasted asparagus and quinoa

Day 2
- Breakfast: Porridge composed of rolled oats, chopped banana, and a scattering of nuts
- Lunch: Tortilla filled with turkey and avocado and whole-wheat bread
- Snack: Crisp slices of carrot accompanied by a dip of hummus
- Dinner: Sauteed tofu served with broccoli and whole-grain rice

Day 3
- Morning meal: Whole-grain toast spread with almond spread and slices of strawberries

- Lunch: Lentil broth with a helping of tossed salad
- Afternoon snack: Cottage cheese with slices of pineapple
- Evening meal: Grilled prawns served with roasted Brussels sprouts and mashed sweet potato.

Day 4
- Morning meal: Greek yogurt construct with granola and fresh fruit
- Mid-day meal: Quinoa dish with chickpeas, cucumber, and feta
- Snack: Sliced apple accompanied by peanut butter
- Evening meal: Roasted chicken breast with green beans and quinoa

Day 5
- Breakfast: Veggie omelet served with a whole-grain loaf
- Lunch: Turkey and veggie stir-fry over brown rice
- Snack: Assorted nuts
- Dinner: Roasted cod with steamed broccoli and quinoa

Week 2:
Day 6:
- For breakfast, overnight oats featuring chia seeds, almond milk, and a mix of fruits.
- For lunch, a delightful combination of spinach and feta-stuffed chicken breast with a side salad.

- As a snack, bite-sized slices of cucumber with tzatziki sauce.
- And for dinner, grilled tofu skewers with sautéed bell peppers and brown rice.

 Day 7
- Breakfast: Multigrain pancakes drizzled with a judicious helping of maple syrup and topped with fresh produce
- Lunch: A wrap of turkey and vegetables served with a side of coleslaw
- Snack: Celery sticks with a dollop of cream cheese
- Dinner: Baked pork loin accompanied by roasted carrots and quinoa

- For breakfast, I blended a smoothie made of spinach, banana, Greek yogurt, and almond milk.
- At lunch, I enjoyed a salad of quinoa and black beans, finished off with some avocado.
- mid-afternoon, I had slices of bell peppers as my snack, accompanied by guacamole.
- For my last meal of the day, I cooked baked chicken thighs with sautéed spinach and brown rice.

Day 9
- Breakfast: Whole-grain waffles with almond spread and chopped strawberries

- Lunch: Lentil and veggie soup plus a dish of tossed greens
- Snack: Cottage cheese with various fruits
- Dinner: Grilled shrimp kebabs with zucchini threads

Week 3:
Day 11 - Morning meal: Greek yogurt sweetened with honey and a few almonds
- Midday meal: Turkey and veggie wok with whole-grain rice
- Treat: Carrot sticks with homemade hummus
- Evening meal: Oven-baked chicken breast accompanied by steamed broccoli and quinoa

Day 12
- Breakfast: Oatmeal topped with banana slices and walnuts
- Lunch: Chicken breast filled with spinach and feta, served with a side salad
- Snack: Cucumber pieces with a side of tzatziki sauce
- Dinner: Cod filet baked to perfection, accompanied by roasted Brussels sprouts and sweet potato.

Day 13
- Breakfast: Scrambled eggs with sautéed spinach and diced tomatoes
- Lunch: Quinoa and black bean medley with slices of avocado

- Snack: Assortment of mixed nuts
- Dinner: Grilled tofu kebabs with bell peppers and steamed brown rice

Day 14
- Breakfast: Whole-grain toast topped with almond spread and diced strawberries
- Lunch: Chargrilled chicken salad with mixed salad greens and balsamic vinaigrette
- Snack: Chopped capsicum with guacamole
- Dinner: Baked pork tenderloin with roasted carrots and quinoa

Day 15
- Breakfast: A milkshake of spinach, banana, Greek yogurt, and almond milk
- Lunch: A bowl of lentil soup alongside a medley of salad greens

- Snack: Apple slices covered in peanut butter
- Dinner: Grilled prawns served on top of zucchini pasta

 Week 4
- Breakfast: Whole-grain pancakes with a small quantity of maple syrup and natural fruit
- Lunch: Turkey and avocado tortilla wrap with wholegrain bread

- Snack: Celery sticks with cheese spread
- Dinner: Baked chicken breasts with fried spinach and brown rice

Day 17
- Breakfast: Veggie omelet accompanied with multi-grain bread
- Lunch: Quinoa bowl comprising of chickpeas, cucumbers, and feta
- Snack: Cottage cheese and an assorted variety of fruit
- Dinner: Oven-baked salmon partnered with asparagus and quinoa

Day 18
- Brekkie: Greek yogurt parfait with muesli & berries

- Lunch: Turkey & veggie stir-fry with brown rice
- Snack: Baby carrots with hummus
- Dinner: Baked chicken breast with steamed broccoli and quinoa

Day 19
- Breakfast: Overnight porridge containing chia seeds, almond milk, and assorted fruit
- Lunch: A chicken breast stuffed with spinach and feta accompanied with a side salad
- Snack: Sliced cucumbers served with tzatziki sauce
- Dinner: Baked pork loin paired with roasted carrots and quinoa

Day20
- Breakfast: Spinach, banana, Greek yogurt, and almond milk smoothie
- Lunch: Grilled chicken salad composed of assorted lettuces and balsamic vinaigrette
- Snack: Apple slices garnished with cinnamon
- Dinner: Grilled tofu skewers alongside bell peppers and brown rice

This month-long meal program offers a mixture of sumptuous and nutritious options while prioritizing blood sugar regulation and overall well being.

Nevertheless, it is essential to bear in mind that personal dietary requirements can vary, mandating consultation with a healthcare specialist or certified nutritionist in order to modify the plan based on individual diabetes type, medication, and lifestyle.

In addition to this nutritional program, regular exercise, vigilant measurement of blood sugar, and any necessary medications are all vital elements of diabetes management. By committing yourself to a nutritious diet, engaging in physical activity, and following your doctor's instructions, you can successfully cope with your diabetes and preserve your overall health and wellness for a prolonged time.

1. Glucose Concentration: In prediabetes, glucose concentrations are escalated but are still not severe enough to satisfy the guidelines for classifying Type 2 diabetes. The two fundamental measures exploited to detect pre-diabetes are:

Fasting Blood Sugar (FBS):A fasting blood sugar level between 100 and 125 milligrams per deciliter (mg/dL) is considered prediabetic.
The Oral Glucose Tolerance Test (OGTT) may be used to detect early signs of prediabetes. A two-hour postprandial

Blood pressure sugar concentration of 140 to 199 mg/dL following the ingestion of a sugar-laden beverage can point to the existence of pre-diabetic conditions.

Prediabetes presents a high likelihood of developing Type 2 diabetes in the future. Those having prediabetes increase their chances of progressing to this particular form of diabetes, although not necessarily unavoidably.

Unlike Type 1 or Type 2 diabetes, prediabetes seldom causes substantial manifestations. A lot of people with prediabetes may be unaware of their affliction until it is identified via general blood testing.

In addition to the heightened chance of Type 2 diabetes, prediabetes is linked with various health dangers. These encompass an amplified likelihood of heart disease and stroke. It is also associated with complications such as high blood pressure and abnormal lipid levels.

Prediabetes is a curable situation, largely due to lifestyle modifications. Making healthier dietary choices, exercising more often, and keeping an optimum weight can significantly reduce the likelihood of developing Type 2 diabetes.

Individuals diagnosed with prediabetes

ought to have consistent medical evaluations. Regular monitoring can assist in monitoring blood glucose concentrations and evaluating overall health. In certain cases, health care professionals may suggest medications to reduce blood sugar concentrations and diminish the danger of diabetes.

 Prediabetes provides a valuable opportunity for people to undertake preventive procedures against Type 2 diabetes. By employing constructive lifestyle changes, such as devouring a healthy diet, participating in daily exercise, and handling tension, individuals have the capacity to postpone or even thwart the development of diabetes.

As it is important to understand, not everyone with prediabetes necessarily proceeds to Type 2 diabetes. It is possible to maximize the odds of preventing or putting off onset through behaving differently. If you are diagnosed with prediabetes, getting close support from a professional medical specialist or educated dietitian can prove to be helpful in controlling your situation and lessening the chances of adverse health outcomes.

Comprehend Your Situation:
It is important to fully grasp the implications of any medical or health

condition. Being aware of the condition can help you to make the most suitable decisions regarding your treatment as well as to manage and navigate any potential lifestyle changes that may become necessary. When first diagnosed, many people can be overcome by feelings of confusion, shock, and fear; however, understanding the condition and the choices available to you is essential to tackling it head-on.

Doing your research into the condition is of paramount importance; make sure to obtain additional information from reliable sources in order to be better informed.

Discussing your diagnosis and available treatments with family, friends, and relevant medical professionals can also be helpful. If decisions have to be made, approaching them from a place of education and knowledge will ensure that you make the best choices for you.

It is normal to be overwhelmed by the effects of any condition, and understanding it gives us the power to manage it. Taking the time to become familiar with the condition can provide a sense of control and allow us to make informed decisions. Accepting accurate, up-to-date information is the key to successfully navigating any medical state.

Become informed about prediabetes, the components which put you at danger, and the potential ramifications. Being knowledgeable is the beginning of effective control.

Discuss your prediabetes diagnosis with a healthcare professional. Pose questions and seek understanding of your particular situation.

Lifestyle modifications are essential in order to lead a healthy life. It necessitates alterations in certain everyday habits that have a direct impact on wellbeing. Diet is one of the most crucial areas to consider when it comes to altering a lifestyle. Eating healthy meals with the right balance of nutrients is vital for a person's physical health. Exercise also plays a significant role in attaining optimal health. Exercise not only has positive effects on physical health but also on mental well being, providing an important means of reducing stress. Lastly, adequate rest and relaxation are crucial; they help the body and mind recover from the toils of the day. In sum, by making necessary lifestyle changes, one can bolster their overall health and wellbeing.

Correction: If you have harmful habits, such as a sedentary lifestyle, bad nutrition, or smoking, address these concerns swiftly.

It is recommended that you take measures toward developing a lasting alteration to your lifestyle. Gradually upsurge physical activity, decrease the amount of refined and sweetened foods in your diet, and contemplate discontinuing smoking if applicable.

A well-balanced diet is essential for overall health. Eating a variety of nutrients from all the food groups can help ensure that your body receives the vitamins and minerals it needs. This includes fruits and vegetables; whole grains; lean proteins, such as fish, legumes, nuts and seeds; low-fat dairy products; and healthy fats, such as olive oil. Additionally, it is important to limit the consumption of added sugars, processed foods, saturated fats and sodium.

A varied and healthy nutrition can provide many benefits. These include a reduced risk of chronic health conditions, such as heart disease, type 2 diabetes and certain types of cancer. Eating a nutritious diet can also increase energy levels, improve mental focus, help control weight and promote better sleep. Establishing healthy eating habits can improve overall quality of life.

It is not difficult to create a nutritious meal plan. Start by choosing whole, unprocessed ingredients; focus on protein-rich foods, such as legumes and fish; add colorful vegetables; and introduce healthy fats to some of your dishes. Try to limit the amount of added sugars and processed foods to promote a healthier diet. Additionally, properly planning meals will facilitate following a balanced nutrition plan.

A balanced diet is necessary for good health. Eating a variety of foods from all the food categories can guarantee that your body is getting the necessary vitamins and minerals. This could include fruits and vegetables, whole grains, lean proteins like fish, legumes, nuts and seeds, low-fat dairy products, and healthy fats like olive oil. However, it is important to limit the consumption of extra sugars, processed foods, high-fat food items and sodium.

Having a varied and healthy diet can bring many rewards. This includes a reduced risk of chronic illnesses such as heart disease, type 2 diabetes and certain types of cancer. Additionally, healthy eating habits can help increase energy levels, sharpen mental focus, manage weight and promote better sleep. Establishing appropriate consuming habits can lead to a better quality of life.

Putting together a nutritious eating plan is not hard. Start by picking out whole unprocessed ingredients, focus on foods high in protein, like legumes and fish, add colorful veggies, and introduce healthy fats to some dishes. Reduce the amount of added sugars andprocessed food items as much as possible to have a healthier diet. Carefully planning meals can aid in following a balanced nutrition plan.

Correction: Correct any unbalanced eating behaviors, including excessive consumption of sugary beverages and processed meals.

Consume a well-rounded diet crammed with unrefined foods, comprising fruits, vegetables, lean meats, whole grains, and beneficial lipids. Take note of portion sizes and attempt for frequent snacks and meals to minimize substantial fluctuations in blood sugar.

Regular physical activity is an essential part of leading a healthy lifestyle. Incorporating exercise into one's daily routine has a multitude of benefits, including improved cardiovascular health, improved mental health, enhanced muscle tone and increased energy levels. Regular physical activity can make an individual look and feel their best.

Taking part in regular exercise can help to reduce the risk of developing heart disease, stroke and some forms of cancer. Exercise increases the heart rate, resulting in improved blood flow throughout the body and the delivery of oxygen to the tissues. This increased blood flow also aids in circulation and metabolism.
Mental wellbeing is also bolstered through regular exercise. Participating in physical activity increases the release of

endorphins, which are the 'feel-good' hormones that trigger positive feelings. This can make a person feel more alert and focused, decrease feelings of anxiety and provide a better sense of self-confidence.

Another major benefit of regular exercise is that it helps to tone and strengthen the body. Exercise aids in building muscle, improving posture and relieving joint pain. This increased muscle tone and strength can help an individual's appearance in addition to providing added functional stability to the body.

Finally, regular exercise can result in

increased energy levels throughout the day. Working out on a regular basis means that an individual's body is in better condition, resulting in better physical performance and quicker reaction time. This can help a person feel more alert and energized throughout their daily routine.

Incorporating regular physical activity into one's life has numerous benefits, such as improved cardiovascular health, psychological wellbeing of, increased muscle tone and strength, and enhanced energy levels. Committing to a regular excrcise regimen is one of the best decisions a person can make for their overall health and wellbeing.

Correction:If you're not physically active, try adding exercise into your regimen.
It is recommended that you strive for 150 minutes of moderate-intensity aerobic activity per week, which may include brisk strolling or riding a bicycle. Moreover, use weight training exercises at minimum two days of the week. Before you initiate a new exercise routine, you should check with your healthcare provider.

Weight maintenance is a crucial aspect of overall health and wellbeing. It is particularly relevant in the context of rising obesity levels around the world. There are several factors that should be considered when trying to sustain a healthy body weight. To begin with, individuals should aim to achieve daily caloric balance. This can help to ensure that the body is neither receiving too little or too much energy, thus helping to preserve a healthy body weight. Secondly, healthy eating choices are also key; opting for nutrient dense, fresh, and unprocessed foods is essential for balanced nutrition. In addition, engaging in regular exercise is also a must, as this helps to increase physical fitness levels and also to burn off excess calories. Last but not least, having the right attitude is paramount - committing to long-term healthy changes is the only way to ensure successful efforts. All in all, with appropriate strategies in place, maintaining a healthy body weight is possible.

Correction: If you are overweight or obese, address excess weight. Suggestion: Aim for a moderate and achievable weight loss through dietary changes and amplified physical activity. Even a minimal drop in weight may dramatically reduce the odds of developing Type 2 diabetes.

Monitoring of Blood Sugar
Blood sugar levels are an essential

aspect of one's health, and regularly assessing them is necessary for the management of diabetes. Monitoring of blood sugar can be done at home or in a healthcare center. Home monitoring enables individuals to keep track of their glucose levels in real-time and be aware of any changes. This is done by using special blood glucose monitors to measure the amount of sugar present in the blood. Checking the levels frequently helps individuals to regulate their diet, adjust medications, and ensure proper diabetes management.

Hospitals and clinics provide sophisticated methods for blood sugar testing which involve a finger-pricking technique to draw a small amount of blood. This blood sample is analyzed using specialized lab equipment to determine the glucose levels. High blood sugar readings may require treatment with medications, lifestyle changes or other measures.

It is important to monitor blood sugar regularly for individuals who are prediabetic, diabetic or have other health problems that affect their glucose levels. Additionally, those who are on insulin treatment should test their blood sugar more often. Doing so will enable a person to know when their numbers are going up or down at any time and act accordingly. By monitoring blood sugar levels, individuals will be able to make adjustments to their diet and/or medications to help manage their condition and avoid any long-term health problems.

Correction: If you've not been monitoring your blood sugar levels, start doing so. It is suggested that you monitor your blood glucose readings as your healthcare professional directs. This gives you the opportunity to track your advancement and get an understanding of the results of your changes in lifestyle on your blood sugar.

If pharmaceuticals are prescribed by a healthcare provider, they should be taken as instructed to maximize efficacy. Adherence to the instructions provided can ensure that the medication taken is beneficial to the person's wellbeing. Taking medicines in the correct amount and at the correct time is critical and may mean the difference between successful treatment and lack thereof. Certain medications could be hazardous if taken in higher than advised quantities and should only ever be taken as prescribed. It is also important to remember that using pharmaceuticals responsibly and correctly can allow people to obtain better short-term and long-term results. Regular reviews of medication should also be done to verify that the treatment remains appropriate and to adjust the dosage if necessary. Ultimately, proper utilization of medication prescribed by a doctor can amplify the outcome of the treatment process.

Correction: If your healthcare professional provides medicine to regulate blood sugar levels, take it as instructed.
It is essential to heed your medical care provider's instructions concerning

medications. Make sure you can recognize when and how to take the medicines and tell them about any repercussions or anxieties you may have, promptly.

Regular examinations are critically important to attending to one's wellbeing. It is highly advocated that one should visit a medical professional on a frequent basis to carry out tests that can detect any underlying conditions or health complications. In addition, this can help with staying ahead of the game and to be aware of any changes in one's health that might be missed without proper examinations. Such services may range from general check-ups, to more specific screenings.

It is highly recommended that one should establish a rapport with a trusted medical practitioner whom they can consult in case of any concerns and have regular test-ups conducted. These check-ups can be done in primary healthcare centres, local hospitals, or even in the comfort of one's own home. Even if one might be feeling perfectly fine, it is important to have these medical examinations done at regular intervals. This will not only give one the assurance that everything is going well, but can also act as a preventative measure for the future.

To conclude, it is essential to make sure that one is having regular check-ups in order to ensure health and wellbeing. Taking advantage of the wide range of services available, one should strive to ensure that such tests are done on a frequent basis. This will provide early detection of any potential health concerns and allow for timely treatment, which could potentially prove life-saving in the long term.

Regular examinations are imperative for maintaining one's health. It is highly recommended that one should form a connection with a medical professional whom they can rely on to carry out periodic assessments that can detect any hidden illnesses or health complications. Such services may include general examinations, as well as more focused screens.

Creating a bond with a reliable medical practitioner is a good idea that would provide one with the ability to inquire if they have any worries and regular tests completed. These check-ups may take place in primary healthcare facilities, hospitals, and even in the comfort of one's home. Even if one feels perfectly fine, it is important to have such medical examinations done on a regular basis. This will not just provide one with the peace of mind that all is going well, but will also act as a form of preventive measure.

it is essential to make sure that one is having regular check-ups in order to sustain their health and well-being. Taking advantage of the various services available, one should strive to guarantee that such tests are done on a periodic basis. This will allow for the early discovery of any potential health problems and allow for prompt treatment, which could end up being life-saving in the future.

Correction: If you've been neglecting regular health check-ups, correct this practice.
It is advised to have regular consultations with your doctor, such as for cholesterol, blood pressure, and kidney functioning tests. These evaluations can help you track your overall health and susceptibility to diabetes.

Stress management is an important life skill to cultivate. Being able to effectively manage the stressors in life can lead to improved physical and mental health. To begin, it is important to recognize situations that prompt feelings of stress.

Once identified, acknowledging the stresses and understanding how they affect the individual is key. Taking proactive steps to reduce the impact of the stressors is the next step; through relaxation activities, adjusting daily routines, and setting realistic goals.

Stress regulation is a necessary life skill to cultivate. Acknowledging the anxieties one experiences and appreciating their effects can be the first move towards understanding them better. Proactive measures must then be taken to tone down their influence. This can include practice of relaxation techniques, modernization of daily routine, and setting reasonable goals. Moreover, building a strong support network further helps to keep the worries in control.

Correction: If you have excessive amounts of stress, address it.
It is advisable to investigate stress-management strategies such as mindfulness, meditation, deep breathing exercises, or leisure activities that can help you to de-stress. Prolonged stress can interfere with your blood sugar levels.

Having a strong support system is essential for mental and emotional health. It is especially important in challenging times, as it can be hard to confront obstacles without the extra assistance of relying on others. Loved ones, such as family members and friends, are typically the cornerstone of any good support system. Having people on your side that are willing to listen and provide words of encouragement can drastically improve a person's wellbeing.

It is additionally beneficial to establish a network of professionals who may be able to provide assistance. Professionals, such as therapists, school counselors, and mentors, can provide valuable insight and advice to help conquer any challenges. Joining groups and organizations, such as those in the online or local community, can also help to tackle a difficulty. For individuals who are especially struggling, there are mental health hotlines available to provide emotional support.

Constructing a reliable support system is integral for making progress and avoiding unnecessary stress. Understanding that there are people around who are willing to help can make it easier to cope through challenging times. Establishing a system of professionals and peers can help to support mental and emotional health and provide necessary aid in times of need.

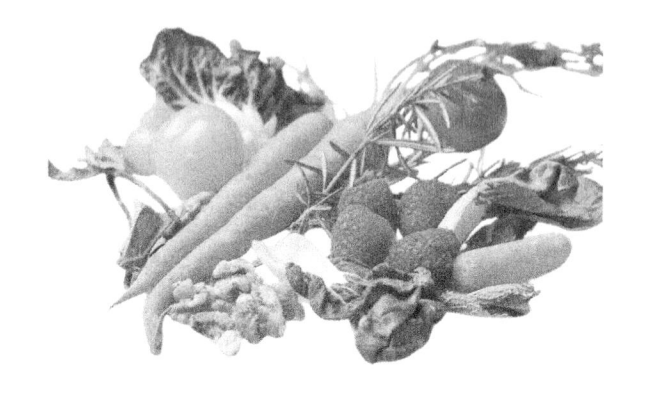

Correction: If you've been treating prediabetes in solitude, consider obtaining help.
I strongly suggest that you share your experience with loved ones or explore joining a diabetes resource group.

Having a trusted circle of people may give you the emotional bolstering and commitment needed to stay on track. Maintaining control over prediabetes is a significant commitment in the long-run, but it brings with it the chance to keep away from or defer the development of Type 2 diabetes, and any ensuing effects. Through making steady, positive modifications to your way of life and partnering closely with your healthcare provider, you can take command of your health and reduce your chances of becoming diabetic.

Printed in Great Britain
by Amazon